W9-BJS-956

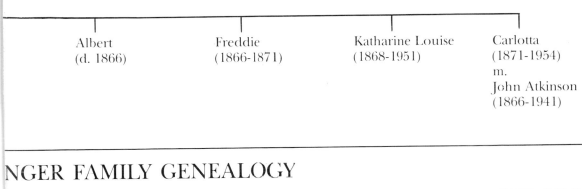

Albert (d. 1866)	Freddie (1866-1871)	Katharine Louise (1868-1951)	Carlotta (1871-1954) m. John Atkinson (1866-1941)

NGER FAMILY GENEALOGY

CHRISTIAN DORFLINGER AND EUGENE DORFLINGER LINES

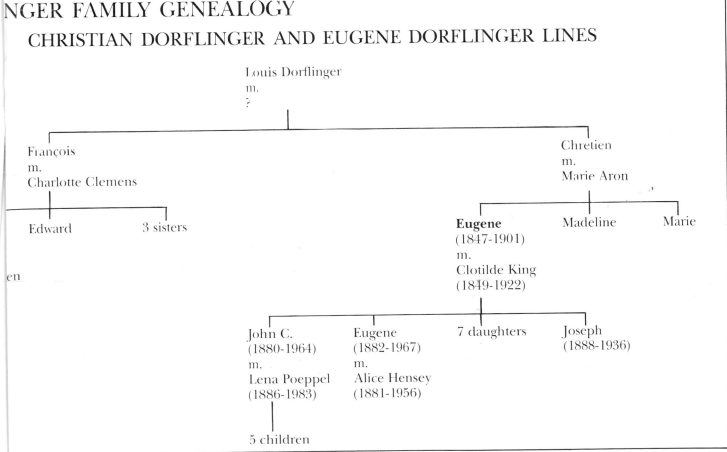

Louis Dorflinger
m.
?

François
m.
Charlotte Clemens

Chretien
m.
Marie Aron

Edward   3 sisters

en

Eugene
(1847-1901)
m.
Clotilde King
(1849-1922)

Madeline   Marie

John C. (1880-1964) m. Lena Poeppel (1886-1983)

Eugene (1882-1967) m. Alice Hensey (1881-1956)

7 daughters

Joseph (1888-1936)

5 children

a pattern of strawberry diamonds, fine diamonds, and hollow
at Seal of the United States, while the glasses are engraved with
r, displayed by the Dorflinger Glass Company at the International
collection of the Philadelphia Museum of Art, the gift Christian

Stoppered decanter and two wine glasses, colorless glass richly cut in
diamonds. The decanter is engraved on one side with a variant of the Gr[...]
two State coats of arms, from a set consisting of thirty eight wines and a decan[...]
Exhibition of 1876, for which the glasshouse won a Certificate of Award. [...]
Dorflinger (photograph by A. J. Wyatt).